WHY I LIKE

Ambassador
Gilbert A. Robinson
(Ret.)

ISBN 978-1467988308
BISAC Category:
Biography & Autobiography;
Presidents and Heads-of-State

Unless otherwise noted, all photos were created by a unit of, or are now the property of, the United States Government.

In memory of
Bernard L. Lewis
co-author of the syndicated
newspaper column
"Why I Like Ike"
on which this book is based.

I would like to acknowledge, with
gratitude, the assistance of Brayton Harris,
Diane Patrick, and John Adams.

CONTENTS
ﻌﻌ

PREFACE
✥❧

In late spring, 1952, while I was lunching with my close friend Bernard Lewis, the subject of "Eisenhower" came up. The General was then being championed as the Republican candidate for president. I told a personal story about Eisenhower, who had visited my Army unit on the Aleutian island of Adak in 1947 when he was Chief of Staff of the Army and I was a young private.

My friend then told me a flattering Eisenhower story of his own, and we got to thinking that other folks might have similar tales to tell. Indeed, Eisenhower was the man of the hour, and we thought that people might like to learn more about the man himself than they might glean from typical press coverage. The campaign slogan was "I Like Ike." We thought, "Why not ask a range of people, 'Why do *you* like Ike?'"

Thus was born a series of small vignettes—each validated by the person who had contributed these stories. These were syndicated to newspapers throughout the nation, including the New York *Daily News* and the Boston *Globe*. The thirty-part series ran for six weeks, five days a week.

These personal anecdotes range from momentary

glimpses of Ike that were highlights in the lives of ordinary Americans to significant incidents that shed light on Eisenhower's character and leadership. These anecdotes also serve as simple examples of his personal appeal and explain why he was a leader loved and respected by so many in the American public. Each of these anecdotes retains the flavor of expression originally used by each individual at the time.

Today, now that the Eisenhower Memorial is underway, people are beginning once again to have an interest in the man. I've pulled out my old files, added brief notes to explain the historical perspective, and offer herewith: "Why I Like Ike."

Gil Robinson

INTRODUCTION
❧❧

The personal recollections in this collection begin in 1941. For today's readers, unfamiliar with the subject, let us begin, briefly, to give him an introduction.

Dwight David Eisenhower—all his life, known as "Ike"—was born in Texas in 1890, but soon his family moved to Abilene, Kansas, which became his home of record. He entered the U. S. Military Academy, West Point, in 1911. He was not the ideal cadet. He collected too many demerits and his grades proved that he was not at the time much interested in academics. He managed—barely—to graduate in the "top half" of his class. He was, however, a standout in athletics (football, fencing, gymnastics) and he showed early leadership skills, serving as junior varsity football coach.

West Point graduation photo, 1915

Mamie and Ike, 1915

Following graduation in 1915, Ike was first assigned to the infantry and, at his first post, he met and married Mamie Doud. They would have two children: Doud Dwight, who died of scarlet fever at age 3, and John Sheldon Doud, who would serve in the Army and Army Reserve. John retired as a brigadier general and was Ambassador to Belgium in the Nixon Administration, 1969-71.

In 1917, when the United States entered World War I, Ike became one of the first officers to command a unit using that newly-introduced weapon, the armored tank. To his great disappointment, the war ended before he and his unit could see combat.

In the summer of 1919, he served as the Tank Corps observer in the first-ever War Department Transcontinental Motor Convoy. Partly for public relations and in part to test

Eisenhower and French tank adopted by the U.S. for World War I.

equipment, it was not a happy journey—56 travel days at an average speed of about six miles an hour, over poor roads, fragile bridges, and with frequent accidents and break-downs. (Later, this experience would lead to President Eisenhower's development, in 1956, of the Interstate Highway System that now bears his name.)

From 1922-24 he had a key assignment as executive officer to the commanding general in the Panama Canal Zone. For the academic year 1925-26, he attended the Command and General Staff College at Ft. Leavenworth, Kansas, where he turned around his academic record, so to speak. He graduated first in a class of 245.

He next served as staff writer for the American Battle Monuments Commission in Washington and Paris, and then was a student at the Army War College. From 1929 to 1933, he was executive officer to the Assistant

Secretary of War. His primary task was to develop a plan to mobilize manpower and materiel for the Army, in the event of future hostilities.

In 1933, he became chief military aide to Army Chief of Staff General Douglas MacArthur—writing speeches, reports, and policy papers. Next, he spent four years with MacArthur in the Philippines, where he sharpened skills that would come in handy when dealing with some of the "difficult" personalities he would encounter later in life.

In 1939, as war approached, Eisenhower had gained broad knowledge of military doctrine, was comfortable working with a range of governments and cultures, and had established a reputation as a good writer and thorough planner. In June, 1941, the newly-promoted Colonel Eisenhower became Chief of Staff for the Third Army.

Soon, he would be on the fast track for promotion and key command assignments with the Arny. He next served as president of Columbia University, then as the first military commander of NATO . . . and then, in 1952 and 1956, he was elected President of the United States. These milestones will be noted in the following narrative.

However . . . when he became a colonel in 1941, Eisenhower rated an orderly . . . and there, we begin.

MICHAEL J. (MICKEY) McKEOGH

❧❧

Orderly / 1941

WHY I LIKE IKE

T he first time I saw General Eisenhower I thought he didn't look much like a soldier. He was just a man in a gray civilian suit with a white shirt and sort of blue tie, and he was eating breakfast with his wife in the kitchen of their house.

I thought he looked more like a retired banker or professional man who had been very athletic a few years before. But he was a colonel, and I, his new orderly, thought, "This is it," and was excited.

He stood up and held out a big hand – a very big hand on the end of a long arm – and then he smiled. There's no use trying to describe that smile. It was just a sincere smile that covered his whole face – not just his mouth, as if he were advertising tooth paste. Somehow, it made me feel better than I had been feeling, on that July day in 1941.

I shook hands with him, and he asked me what my name was.

"Private Michael James McKeogh, Sir," I said. He sort of shook his head at that, but he kept on smiling. "I know that," he said. "I mean, what do they call you?"

"Mickey, sir," I said,

He kept on smiling and this time he nodded. "O. K., Mickey," he said. "That's what it will be from here on out."

He sort of nodded at his wife then and said, "All right, you take care of things around here – and of her, too."

I said I'd certainly try to, and he said he thought I'd do and then he sat down to finish his breakfast. I went to work around the house. I was pretty much keyed up still, but I thought he'd be a nice guy to work for – even if he was a colonel.

Suddenly his smile flashed across my mind, and I wondered if a colonel with such a smile could ever be a general. Not from what I heard about generals. No – I figured I was pretty well off working for the colonel with the big smile – Colonel Dwight David Eisenhower. ■

Sergeant McKeogh would serve with Eisenhower for the duration of World War II.

Eisenhower's true potential was soon recognized, and he did not remain a colonel for long; he became a brigadier general in September 1941, major general in March 1942, lieutenant general in July.

He was appointed commander of all Allied forces for the invasion of North Africa in November.

By February, 1943, he wore the four stars of a general while commanding the invasion of Sicily and Italy. That December, he took over at Supreme Headquarters of the Allied Expeditionary Forces (SHAEF) to prepare for the invasion of northern Europe.

MARTY SNYDER
❧❧

Mess Sergeant / 1942

WHY I LIKE IKE

During World War II, I was Mess Sergeant to the Supreme Headquarters of General Eisenhower for more than three and a half years. I'll never forget the first time he inspected the mess hall and kitchen.

Other officers I had known went through with all the pomp and ceremony of Napoleon, sticking their white gloves into every nook and cranny looking for dust.

Eisenhower, instead, inspected with a thorough knowledge of what he was doing. He looked into the pots, tasted the food, asked what was on the menu for the troops. He checked the storage of food in refrigerators. He went right to the heart of the problem, checking all the things that really counted. There was nothing "chicken" about him.

He himself was not a fussy eater, although he loved food and was an excellent cook – as I found out to my chagrin.

Knowing the conditions he had to work under, and the strain on him, I tried to take extra pains to prepare foods he liked. I knew he liked baked beans New England style. One evening I put the beans in individual crocks, and since our mess had no fire going during the night, I took the beans to a bakery and left them there to bake slowly overnight.

The next day I served the beans at lunch. I stood around to see how he liked them. After lunch he approached me and said: "Marty, I thought you were a chef. These are not New England baked beans. You put tomato in them. *Real* New England baked beans are made with sorghum syrup or black molasses . . ."

I bowed my head in shame as the General reeled off the recipe. Next time, the beans were a success even though I had to search every Quartermaster center in Europe to find the right ingredients.

When we first moved headquarters to France, the local people presented the General with a cow, so that he would have fresh milk. That night three of us, all city boys, went to the stall where "Betsy" was kept, to see if we could figure out how to get milk for the General's breakfast. "Betsy" would not cooperate. We were absorbed in our

efforts – and getting absolutely no place – when we heard
an amused voice boom out on the other side of the stall:

"Need a hired hand there?" It was the Supreme Commander himself.

P.S. The next morning we all had fresh milk. ∎

QUENTIN REYNOLDS

❧❧

Journalist / 1943

WHY I LIKE IKE

During World War II the Germans' psychological warfare division started rumors to the effect that General Eisenhower was Jewish. They were trying to take advantage of what they thought was latent anti-Semitism among our troops. It is significant that their propaganda misfired. The GIs just laughed it off.

Somehow the stories took hold at home and many people in our own country think that it is true. Being the man he is, General Eisenhower has never confirmed or denied the rumors. He didn't confirm it because it wasn't true, but he didn't deny it because he felt that he wouldn't be ashamed of being Jewish if he were.

Once I was present in London when Ike got a letter from his brother, Milton. He read it, snorted, and showed it to me,

"I was at a cocktail party here in Washington," wrote Milton "given by one of those real old dowagers. She said very nicely to me, "You must come from a fine family, young man. You have an important job here and your brother is leading our troops abroad and I understand another brother is a banker. What a pity it is that you

Eisenhowers are Jewish!"

"I looked at her, sighed unhappily, and said, 'Ah, madam, what a pity it is that we aren't.'"

General Eisenhower put the letter down, laughed, and said "Wasn't that a wonderful answer to give the old battle axe? I'd forgotten that there were people like that still in the world." ■

18

The invasion of northern Europe began on the beaches of Normandy, France on June 6, 1944—designated then and remembered yet today as "D-Day."

Troops landing on "Omaha Beach," Normandy, France, June 6 1944.

MAJOR GENERAL
ROYAL B. LORD
&❧&

Deputy Chief of Staff, SHAEF / 1944

WHY I LIKE IKE

As former Deputy Chief of Staff to General Eisenhower, I admired him for never allowing friendship to stand in the way of his duty to public interest.

In London a month before D-Day, a Major General who was a classmate and close friend of Eisenhower's attended a party at the Hotel Claridge. The biggest military secret in the world at the time was the date of the invasion of Europe. During the party an attractive woman was talking with the general and brightly remarked: "Do you think D-Day will come in the early part of June?" To which the general replied:

"You won't be far from wrong."

Ike heard about the incident, sent for the general, and said to him:

"Every soldier who violates the rules, whether he is an enlisted man or officer, regardless of his relationship to me, will be given equal treatment."

Ike broke him to a colonel and sent him home in disgrace. He followed this principle of equal treatment many times, including the famous case in which he relieved

General Patton from command in Italy, and then despite opposition made him an Army Commander in Europe, where he attained tremendous success.

More often than not, however, Ike meets his problems gently, and not sternly. Like brilliant men throughout history, he has the knack of making people see his point of view.

Once, at SHAEF, Ike was discussing the world situation with a distinguished visitor from home. A certain point was reached in the discussion and the visitor straightened up in his seat, and you could tell that he was about to throw a curve ball.

"Should we keep giving money to Europe," he said, "when they aren't helping themselves?"

Ike looked at him and slowly answered:

"If you and another fellow are crossing a river, and you discover suddenly that you are being swept downstream to destruction, and he loses his oar – do you give up or do you keep on rowing?" ■

Paris had been liberated by the end of August, 1944 and the American and British forces were moving forward.

American troops passing the Arc de Triomphe, Paris, August 1944.

BERNARD L. LEWIS
❖❖

Commander, Information Control Division / 1944

WHY I LIKE IKE

I served under Eisenhower in Germany. Way under. I never even got to see the man, but he did one thing that affected me which I will never forget.

My outfit was Information Control Division. Our mission was to turn all media of communications – newspapers, radio stations, etc., – over to anti-Nazi Germans. The German people still believed Hitler's lies, and needed to be brought up to date on recent history. We needed newspapers, edited and produced by reliable Germans, for Germans.

The difficulties were fantastic. Property control laws were weak. Most printing plants and radio stations were bombed out and had to be rebuilt. We needed parts, and our occupation zone was criss-crossed with tactical troops and military government forces who "controlled" areas and had the local printing plant working day and night on regimental histories, etc.

Some of our men, in an effort to accomplish their mission, began forging orders and stealing equipment at gun-point from both Americans and Germans. We knew this could only lead to serious trouble.

One day I ran into a situation in which the labor of weeks was jeopardized by one uncooperative officer. I appealed everywhere, in vain.

In my desperation, I thought of Eisenhower. Somehow I felt that he would understand. If I could only talk to him. Then I thought of the idea of writing to him. Crazy, but I did it, explaining my problem like one friend to another.

After I mailed the letter, I backtracked and tried to get it out of the mailroom. But it was too late. I had committed a cardinal army sin, by defying channels.

An envelope arrived for me two weeks later. In it was a letter to me and individual memoranda addressed "To Whom It May Concern," one for each of our men, explaining the bearer's mission and "requesting" cooperation. Three weeks later the first newspaper in Bavaria was licensed. The "request" for cooperation had worked. Why not, after all, each memorandum was personally signed:

"Eisenhower." ■

American machine gun crew in Aachen, October 1944.

GENERAL
RAYMOND S. McLAIN
❧❧

Commander, U. S. Army XIX Corps
(Armored) / October, 1944

WHY I LIKE IKE

The following I think indicates the simplicity and at the same time, the great leadership of General Eisenhower.

I had just taken command of the XIX Corps, at that time, October 1944, fighting at Aachen. A few days after I had assumed command, General Eisenhower visited my command post in order to inspect the troops. He always insisted on going out and visiting the troops nearest the front lines. We had one battalion in small woods which protected them from observation by the enemy.

It was a very rainy, muddy day when General Eisenhower arrived. We rode out to the location of the troops in a jeep and climbed up through an orchard to the edge of the woods in which the troops were assembled. General Eisenhower stepped on a platform and made a very short and interesting talk to the troops in which he made them understand that he knew the circumstances, difficulties, and hardships they were undergoing. It appealed to the soldiers very much and they did something which soldiers seldom do. When he had concluded, they clapped and cheered him.

He stepped off the platform on to the muddy ground and his feet slipped out from under him and he, the Supreme Commander, fell right on the seat of his pants. It was a little too much for the soldiers to hold themselves. They let out a yell and cheered again. I am certain that if this had been some other commanders whom I have known in my military career, I would have faced a court martial for permitting lax discipline or else "taken off" for the German lines quickly.

That was not the case with General Eisenhower, however. He got up, gave his broad smile to the troops and waved his hand at them. The troops roared their approval.

I am sure that they would have followed him any-where in the world that he could have asked them to go. ■

In December, 1944, Eisenhower was promoted to the five-star rank of General of the Army.

By the following March, the Allies were well inside Germany. The Germans surrendered on May 7, 1945:"Victory in Europe (V-E) Day."

Eisenhower became military governor of the U.S. Occupied Zone. The Russian army, which had moved into Germany from the East, created their own Zone of occupation.

GENERAL LUCIUS D. CLAY
֍֎

Eisenhower's Deputy / 1945

WHY I LIKE IKE

Less than a month after the defeat of Germany, I accompanied General Eisenhower to Berlin, where he was to join the Commanders-in-Chief of our Allies in signing the documents providing for the control of Germany.

The ceremony was scheduled for noon. We landed, at Templehof, in the morning. General Eisenhower was received with appropriate honors by a Soviet contingent of troops.

Well past noon, we were served lunch. We had so far only been received by minor Soviet officials.

Several more hours were lost when the Soviets objected to a minor clause in the agreement, which had already been confirmed by their government. We settled this to their satisfaction, and it was at five o'clock that we finally met Marshal Zhukov, Andrei Vishinsky and the main Soviet group.

The formal ceremony was concluded in a few minutes, and Marshal Zhukov led us to the porch, where wine and vodka were served, after which he invited us to be his guests at a banquet. General Eisenhower reminded him that he had been in Berlin for many hours for a simple ceremony and that, while he would be glad to attend the banquet, it was necessary for him to leave at six o'clock as he had to return to Frankfurt that day.

At the banquet, there were the usual rounds of toasts of vodka. Marshal Zhukov then rose to his feet and toasted the four heads of state, extending a welcome to the three Western Commanders-in-Chief.

General Eisenhower was turning over in his mind the events of the day, the hours of delay, which he did not believe conformed to the dignity of his position as a representative of the United States. When he rose to respond, he spoke warmly of the victorious Red Army and its accomplished, military leaders, but he closed his response quickly, expressing regret that the long delay had prevented an earlier start as he now had to thank his hosts and say good-bye.

I am sure that the Russians did not expect him to leave on schedule and that it proved an effective lesson.

34

Henceforth their appointments with him were kept as sedulously as he kept his own. ■

June 5, 1945: Marshal Georgy Zhukov, center, pouring a toast for Field Marshal Bernard Montgomery, with Eisenhower looking on.

The month after V-E Day, Eisenhower enjoyed a triumphant "homecoming" tour in the United States with grand parades in New York and Washington and an enthusiastic welcome at his home town, Abilene, Kansas.

CHARLES M. HARGER
❦❦

Editor, *Abilene Reflector-Chronicle* / 1945

WHY I LIKE IKE

I have known Dwight Eisenhower for many years. As Editor of the *Abilene Reflector-Chronicle*, I have watched the progress of his career with more than casual interest. My liking for him stems from the fact that he knows no "swank" – the self-importance with which some prominent persons make themselves offensive.

Some people believe his friendliness and grin are "put on," like the politician who suddenly takes to kissing babies. Remember, I knew this man before he became famous – and I assure you that he has not changed a bit. He was just as warm and friendly as he is now.

During the height of World War II, when he was commanding all the Allied forces in Europe, he wrote me that when he came home he hoped his friends would not address him by any fancy titles, but they should call him "Ike" and added, "If they do not I shall feel greatly hurt." He came home and they called him Ike, and he felt comfortable because of it.

On June 4, 1945, at the homecoming celebration here in Abilene 30,000 persons poured into this 6,000 population town and he was besieged by governors, congressmen, prominent citizens of all types. Yet he took time out to visit an old friend now bedfast, to call on a teacher of his elementary school days, and to go down the street to the little cafe where he and his boyhood cronies used to gather, and shake hands with the proprietor and chat for a little while.

A friend gave a luncheon and with old time familiarity he insisted on going to the kitchen and seeing what the waitresses had for the table. They were delighted. Those are the things that men with "swank" do not do. He does these things naturally and unconsciously, and that is why he is loved wherever he is. ■

DAVID G. CHASE

Childhood Friend / 1946

WHY I LIKE IKE

I remember a discussion Ike and I had when we were both young men. We met in a restaurant just after he finished his first year at West Point. At the time I was driving a delivery wagon for a grocery store – and earning real money.

"Ike," I said, "I'm going to get me a farm. I think there is a good future here in the Middle West for farmers."

Ike always liked farming, and he agreed with me.

"Why don't you get a farm, Ike," I said. "You're going to put in ten more years getting an education, and I will have my fortune made and you'll still be in school."

I had been doing all the talking, and Ike the listening. But at that point he broke loose, and this is what he said as clearly as I can remember it:

"Dave, when I was in grade school and studying history, it became plain to me that what our country needs is more young men with an education. There is a time in the future when more and better leadership will be needed, and it is my desire to be able to serve the people of the United States."

When Ike came home to Abilene recently I was walking on the street and there he was, we hadn't seen each other in a long time, and we grabbed each other like the old friends we are. A photographer snapped the picture, and I understand it has gone all over the country. What they don't know is that he said to me:

"Dave, where can I get a hundred acres of wheat land that I won't go broke on?" I told him I would fix him up on that, and I have got the county commissioners of Dickinson County to lease him one hundred acres of the county farm. I will be agent – and will mail the lease to Ike.

It looks like, of the two of us, Ike has made out better. He not only has gotten the education and has served the people of the United States – but now he's a farmer, too. ■

November, 1945. Eisenhower was appointed Chief of Staff of the Army, to serve until the spring of 1948.

MRS. ROBERT P. PATTERSON
❧❧

Spouse, Secretary of War / 1946

WHY I LIKE IKE

Whenever anyone mentions the word "tact," I think of Eisenhower.

My husband and I were with him in Chicago on the first Army Day [April 6] after World War II. At the Chicago station we heard the first spontaneous chorus of "Hi, Ike," which was to follow us through the day.

Before the parade, we went to the Blackstone Hotel, where a good welcome and a seven-course luncheon awaited us. On the dais, I was seated at Eisenhower's left.

We were talking pleasantly when we became conscious of the waiter standing behind us, still and majestic, like a guard at Buckingham Palace. When he saw that he had the General's attention, he bowed from the waist, bringing into view the platter in his hand.

On it was the most tremendous baked potato I have ever seen.

"General," the waiter said, impressively, "We remembered you like baked potatoes."

He then laid it with great respect on Eisenhower's plate. The General grinned with pleasure and thanks.

We went on talking a minute, until I noticed Eisenhower glancing around. He satisfied himself that the coast was clear and said:

"I know all of you want some of this wonderful baked potato,"

Quick as a flash, he winked at us and placed large forkfuls on our plates. In a few minutes – to the pride and delight of the waiter – there was the General calmly finishing the last of that tremendous potato. ■

Portrait of General Eisenhower, by Thomas E. Stephens

THOMAS E. STEPHENS

❧❧

Portrait painter / 1946

WHY I LIKE IKE

We have heard a great deal about Churchill as an amateur artist, but not many people know that General Eisenhower is also an excellent painter. How he became an artist suggests qualities of genius, for it was typical of the way extremely brilliant people master intricate subjects.

I have been privileged to paint Ike's portrait more times than any other artist, including the canvas in the National Gallery in Washington, D. C., and the one at the U. S. Military Academy at West Point. Soon after the war, I was doing a portrait of him at his residence in Fort Meyer, Virginia. He watched and watched and finally burst out with:

"By golly, I'd like to try that."

I needed some rest, because he is difficult to paint. His expressions change so swiftly,

"Why don't you try?" I invited. That was all he needed.

"Fix me up a canvas, Moaney," he said to his

sergeant. Back, in a flash came Sgt. John Moaney with an old piece of canvas tacked to a board.

With enthusiasm Ike took the canvas. He had Mrs. Eisenhower sit for him and he started a portrait of her.

Without a word of instruction from me, and with tremendous intensity, Ike worked on that canvas for many hours. Finally, he held up the canvas, It was a remarkable picture of Mrs. Eisenhower, with a primitive but very decorative feeling. Ike was launched as an artist. He has never taken a lesson, but he stores up very technical questions which he gives me whenever we meet.. He takes criticism in a wholesome manner, but is independent when he thinks he is right, as this will serve to illustrate.

I sat behind him in Paris this April as he painted a portrait of General Montgomery from a photo and memory. Occasionally I made a criticism and he would nod his head and say: "Yes, you're right."

At the end of two hours I said, "Leave it. It looks very good."

"I think it's too light," he replied.

We disagreed about it, and several weeks later when I saw him in New York I asked him if he did as I advised. He looked at me with a triumphant grin, and said:

"No. I made it warmer in color, and I gave it to the old man [Montgomery] and he was delighted with it!" ■

Dwight Eisenhower portrait of Bernard L. Montgomery.
Now in the Royal Art Collection, UK.

LESLIE R. STEWART
❦❦

Soldier / 1947

WHY I LIKE IKE

I was on Adak after World War II. It was an island, treeless, womanless, an earthquake-ridden hunk of cold and wet volcanic ash stuck out in the Bering Sea between Alaska and Siberia

To say that we hated Adak is putting it mildly. Put 5000 American GIs on an island like that and you've got more griping than you ever heard in your life

One day, in 1947 it was, I have no idea of the months in that place, we heard that General Eisenhower himself was coming to inspect the island. We polished up that place so a white glove could be put on it anyplace.

The day Ike was to arrive, I was one of the guys being drilled by a captain in front of the reviewing stand from which the General would look us over. He drilled us until we were ready to drop. He kept saying:

"Now remember who this is! Stand at attention!"

Eisenhower's party finally arrived. The men stood at button-busting attention as the anthem was played. Then Ike smiled, "All right, men, at ease ... break ranks, come on up here so you can hear me better."

The captain's jaw dropped to his knees. The men

rushed up to the general, and he started to talk . . . and in the middle of it he pulled a prize boner!

"Now you men on Umnak . . . " he said. Umnak was hundreds of miles away. This gave the average GI a chance to snicker or laugh or actually take advantage of the General's informality and shout out loud, "Not Umnak – Adak."

But there wasn't a sound. Where we were didn't seem important anymore, for even though others had "briefed" us before, Ike's talk made us sense the importance not of where we were, but of why we were there. ■

Adak, Aleutian Islands, Alaska.

The 1948 presidential election was looming in the near future, and the co-founder of the Young & Rubicam advertising agency launched a "Draft Eisenhower" movement.

Planting seeds . . . to be harvested four years later.

JOHN ORR YOUNG
❧❧

Former Chairman, Young & Rubicam / 1947

WHY I LIKE IKE

In 1947 I started a one-man crusade to draft Eisenhower for the Presidency, yet I never met General Eisenhower until just recently, and the circumstances are interesting . . . I'll tell you about them in a moment.

I have often been asked why I have worked so persistently for the Eisenhower "crusade." Why? Because it is a crusade, we desperately need Eisenhower's obvious abilities, intellectual capacity, spirituality, personality, background, and innumerable other attributes. Here is the man for the job. Back in 1947 I felt that millions of fellow Americans might agree, so I reasoned, let's get him to run and help him win. I put a simple paid advertisement in the newspaper of my town, Westport, Connecticut, stating my faith in Eisenhower and calling for cooperation. That "grass roots" beginning snowballed into a national advertising campaign which I discontinued after the proper political organizations were set up and functioning.

Never during this crusade have I sought to benefit myself in favors, office or profits; and that is why I was in no rush to meet him.

When the Connecticut delegation called on him in

June at his Columbia University home, there were about a hundred people watching, and people milling about him on the sidewalk.

I was in back of the crowd, quietly taking it all in. Governor John Lodge, who was standing with Eisenhower, happens to be a very tall man and he spotted me. He called over the heads of the crowd and motioned me to come forward. When I did so for the first time I was face to face with the man who has occupied my thoughts for four years.

"General Eisenhower," Governor Lodge said, "here is the man who started the Eisenhower campaign back in 1947 in the state of Connecticut."

In the confusion, I didn't hear what Ike said, but he grabbed my hand warmly and his smile seemed to say, "I don't know whether I ought to thank you or not for having started this thing." ■

As his tour as Chief-of-Staff was winding down, the General was persuaded to draft his account of the war in Europe . . .

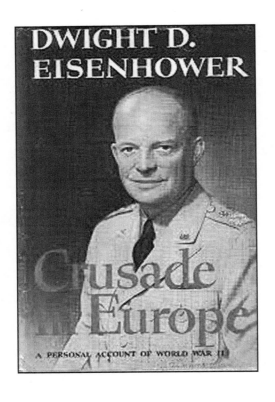

KENNETH McCORMICK
᪥

Editor-in-Chief, Doubleday / 1948

WHY I LIKE IKE

General Eisenhower wrote his 559-page book, "Crusade in Europe," in about four months by dictating to a stenographer. He seldom referred to any documents, and just had some war maps in front of him. He remembered almost every detail of the world's greatest war. He has a mind that retains every impression to which it is exposed.

During the staggering task of writing and editing the "Crusade in Europe" manuscript the whole world wanted to ask him questions. Both the Democrats and Republicans wanted to draft him and were feeling him out. But he isolated himself, concentrated completely on the one subject, and worked steadily from 9 am to midnight with only two interruptions in the entire 14 weeks!

He adheres to principles with the same strength with which he concentrates on ideas. When he was in command in North Africa a U. S. General asked permission to have a private dinner with some captured German generals and sit and chat about strategy. Ike would not even consider it.

"I don't think war is a game," he once told me. "I don't belong to the school that believes the generals can be above the mess, and act as if they belonged to some superior society."

"I never spoke to a German general, except to Jodl, and that was to order him to my office to be sure he understood the terms of the surrender." ∎

In May, 1948, Eisenhower left active duty to accept a position as president of Columbia University, New York City.

He would remain actively involved with the job for not quite two years.

Low Memorial Library, Columbia University, New York City.

MISS LYNN STANTON
❦❦

TWA Hostess / 1948

WHY I LIKE IKE

One day I was called in by my superiors at TWA. I was told that I was to be one of two hostesses on the plush plane "Star of Kansas," which was to fly General Eisenhower from Washington to Kansas City, and then to New York. Both Sally Drury and I were thrilled at the prospect.

General Eisenhower had just stepped out of uniform, and he seemed very tired. TWA had printed up a special menu, and had prepared a wonderful meal. The menu said: "Homecoming Flight of Mr. Dwight D. Eisenhower."

Ike looked at it, let out a roar, and immediately started showing it to everyone on the plane. It apparently was the first time he had ever seen the "Mr." in print. He seemed to feel a little better after that.

He was charming and gracious on the trip, and it's wonderful the way he gives you his undivided attention when he talks with you. But I thought that might be just a knack he had acquired, and that he would forget us immediately.

Not so. At the airport when we were ready for the flight to New York he spotted us in the crowd and came over especially to greet us.

I didn't see this myself, but on the plane they talked about the fact that as Ike was nearing the plane a photographer kept backing up in front of him trying to get a picture. A young boy got in his way, and the photographer in his eagerness pushed him out of the way, and the boy spun to the ground. Ike saw this, and walked quickly to the boy's side, bent down, put his arm around him and lifted him up.

"He had no business doing that to you," Ike said.

It's that quality I sensed in him during the trip – a sincere and unusual interest in people, whether they are big or small. ■

The Pentagon, headquarters of the Department of Defense.

W. WALTER WILLIAMS
✦✦

Chairman, Council on Economic Development / 1948

WHY I LIKE IKE

In the fall of 1948 I was a speaker at a luncheon at which Ike was to be presented with the Sales Executive Club "Clasped Hands" award. The general was sitting at my side as I arose to speak. I began my remarks by relating an anecdote which I had heard about him. This is the story I told:

"It seems that when Ike was in the Pentagon, he was visited by a delegation of ladies. When they started to leave, being a courteous man, he escorted them through the maze of corridors out to the main entrance and down the steps. He opened the door of their car and saw them safely on their way before reentering the building.

"He retraced his steps, in the direction from which he thought he had come but couldn't seem to find the way. The corridors were endless and empty and the man who had guided millions of troops across Europe was hopelessly lost, and wandering aimlessly. Soon he heard the sound of someone walking down the corridor.

"It was a major. The General stood in front of him, feet apart, with hands on hips, and said: 'I'm Ike Eisenhower--and I'm lost!'"

I heard Ike laugh uproariously when I finished the anecdote, so I knew it was true. When I returned to my place, he leaned over smiling and firmly encircled my shoulders with his arm, in a gesture of friendship.

Later he got to his feet and in his talk mentioned my anecdote, and admitted that it was true.

"But, I'd like to add something to it," he said. "That Major looked at me astonished, and embarrassed, and pointed to a door not fifteen feet away and said timidly:

"But General, there's your office!" ∎

*Williams later served as Eisenhower's
Under Secretary of Commerce
(the position would be "Deputy Secretary," today).*

ELI GINZBERG

Professor of Economics, Columbia University / 1948

WHY I LIKE IKE

Because of General Eisenhower, I once turned down $500,000. It happened this way:

Ike had been appointed and accepted his post at Columbia, but had not yet taken over his new duties. General Snyder, now Eisenhower's physician, General Eisenhower, and I had lunch together. General Snyder had been Assistant Inspector General of the Army, and I had served with the army as a manpower and logistics expert, and was then with Columbia. During lunch Ike brought up the subject of his concern over the fact that Selective Service had rejected five million of the 18 million men screened during World War II.

"We'd better learn, and do something about that," he said. That was the beginning of the Conservation of Human Resources project, which I now head at Columbia.

It didn't take form until Ike took over at the university. He personally contacted fifty people in public life, getting their opinions and support. Then the project got under way, in collaboration with the Department of Defense. Ike had conceived the plan so that the government would supply much of the information, Columbia much of the brains and manpower, and industry most of the money.

And that's where the $500,000 comes in.

James C. Forrestal was head of the Department of Defense, and when he heard of the project he was so enthused that he immediately offered to have the Department of Defense support it in full.

But Ike was convinced that it was proper for American industry to have a part in this project, so he sent me to Washington to explain to Forrestal why it would be best not to accept the offer.

I don't know of any other man who could turn down so easily a half-million dollars because of the principle that universities should get their own funds and not become dependent on government. ∎

Over many years, the Conservation of Human Resources Project would address a wide range of manpower issues —including problems with the individual performance of soldiers, management and labor relations, health care, career guidance, and race relations.

HENRY J. CARMAN
❧❧

Dean, Columbia College--the college of
Arts and Sciences at Columbia University / 1948

WHY I LIKE IKE

Just prior to General Eisenhower's inauguration as President of Columbia University, Columbia College established its Forum on Democracy. Held annually, representatives from approximately one hundred leading private preparatory and public high schools from the northeastern United States are three-day guests of the College. The President of the University or someone designated by him is the lead-off person who sparks the entire conference.

On this particular occasion, which was also Lincoln's birthday, it was logical that the General should be the keynoter, and as Dean of the College at that time it was my pleasant duty to invite him to give the opening address. I called on him in person, for as everybody knows he is a very approachable person and likes to discuss matters face to face. After explaining my mission he said "Harry, this proposal to hold an annual conference of this kind is a splendid idea but unfortunately I have an important meeting in Washington on February 12th."

"I'm terribly sorry for we want so much to have you with us on this occasion" was my reply.

He pondered for a moment and then asked "What time did you have me scheduled for?"

"Eleven o'clock," I replied.

Again there was a moment of silence and then he exclaimed, "All right, Harry, I'll be here; I'll come up by plane, and then rush back to the meeting. This has to do with youth and with the future of our country and I'm not going to miss it. I'll be here at five minutes of eleven."

When the appointed day came, he was there. "Terribly sorry Mr. President, to add this chore to your many burdens," was my greeting.

"No burden at all, I want to be in on this."

The auditorium was packed to capacity and photographers were everywhere. I introduced him at once and the ovation was thunderous. He spoke extemporaneously for seventeen minutes, and when he finished, what he had said was so perfectly expressed that it could have been sent to the printer without change – even so much as a comma. And even though he was scheduled to return to Washington at once to resume the important meeting in which he was participating, he was not so rushed that he did not have time for a handshake and a personal word for the young men who, deep in their souls, had been stirred and inspired by a great American. ■

PATRICK KENNEDY
❦

Gardener, Columbia University / 1948

WHY I LIKE IKE

I am one of the gardeners at Columbia. When Ike took over the job as president of the university, he called all the working people together in the library. It was a large group – we were all in our working clothes – some maids, some cooks, maintenance workers, etc.

He made a short speech, but we all appreciated it because we knew he didn't have to do a thing like that. I remember he said something like this:

"Each individual has a job to do, and no matter what it is we are all equal, and one job depends on the next . . . "

When he left, he said with that wonderful grin of his:

"Now if you fellows ever meet me around the campus, don't ignore me just because I come from the sticks."

The reason I called him Ike, is that I have his own permission to do so. He talked to the maintenance workers once and said:

"Call me by my first name, Ike, and if I know yours I'll do the same."

He is probably the first college president on record

who ever invited the workers to use his first name.

Once a friend of mine was mopping up Ike's office when he came in unexpectedly and obviously busy. My friend tried to speed up the work, but Ike put his hand on his shoulder and told him to "take it easy."

Once I was shoveling snow off the steps of the Low Memorial Library. My head was down and I was just shoveling away, when I sensed somebody standing behind me.

I was blocking the path, and no one could get ahead of me until I finished. I turned around – and there was Ike, one of the busiest men in the world. He smiled at me and said:

"I have plenty of time." ∎

ALPHONSE FALISE

❦❧

Head, Columbia University Security Force / 1948

WHY I LIKE IKE

As the head of Columbia's security force, I have seen a great deal of Ike. I think he is one of the most humane men in the world, one who always considers the other fellow. He doesn't like to see people pushed around.

Once I saw a photographer gruffly push some people aside to get a picture when he had ample time and opportunity to get it without being rude, It annoyed Ike terribly. At the right moment, he approached the photographer and said:

"I try hard to be decent, and I'd like you to be decent, too."

He has an unlimited amount of patience with people and tries to do little things for them. He never fails when asked a question, and gives a decent answer even when the question is nebulous and hazy. Of all the multitude of questions I have seen him asked, and the autographs he is requested to sign, I have never seen him brush anyone off, no matter whether the people were big or small.

No matter who his guests are, he looks after them

personally. I remember when the Shah of Iran's party visited him, he looked after their coats himself.

I have worked for Pinkerton, and was in the army for 29 years, so it is incredible to me that Ike has never once told me what my duties are. I believe he lets people observe for themselves, and come to their own conclusions,

One little thing about him is very revealing to me.

On many occasions he has asked me to get some small item for him, or to do something for him, but, with a twinkle in his eyes, he will say:

". . . if you can get it without using my name."

He knows who he is and what his name means to people, yet he doesn't want any favors. He only wants it if someone else can get it, too. ■

Eisenhower Leadership Patch, Boy Scouts of America.

PHILIP FOWLER, JR.

✎✎

Boy Scout Inductee / 1949

WHY I LIKE IKE

I became 12 years old in 1949, and joined the Boy Scout movement. It was all very quiet and normal – and all of a sudden I got a call from Scout Headquarters. I was the 500,000[th] boy to become a scout in New York City and I was to be inducted at a Dawn Patrol Breakfast at the Waldorf-Astoria by none other than General Eisenhower.

In the three weeks before the breakfast I had visions of a stiff, gruff military man coldly pinning on my tenderfoot badge. My knees were knocking together when I finally met him on the stage where the ceremony was to take place.

My eyes swept in the 1,000 guests, the television cameras, newsreel cameras, photographers, and General Eisenhower – and I almost turned around and ran. I kept saying to myself: "And all I did was join the Boy Scouts."

Evidently General Eisenhower sensed my feelings because he looked at me, then came over and started talking. He said he was more nervous than I was, and that we would comfort each other. He was friendly and kind – entirely different than I had pictured him. Because of the various cameramen, we had to repeat the act of putting on the pin time and time again. He was patient and kept joking with me.

Then he made a short, unprepared speech which was really terrific. He told about the time his own son was in the Boy Scouts and taking his 14-mile hike. Mrs. Eisenhower sent General Eisenhower to catch up with his son in a station wagon, and offer him some orange juice. His son refused because it was against the rules.

"I never told my mother or my wife," General Eisenhower said. "I told nobody until today that *I* drank the orange juice."

Everyone loved him, and right after the ceremony throngs crowded up to shake his hand. My mother, father and sister were there, and as he shook hands with them he spied my sister hanging shyly in the background. He said in a booming voice, "Well, this must be Sis." This shocked us all, because that's exactly what she has always been called. He made a big fuss over her and made her feel very good.

As though all that wasn't enough, I later received

a letter from him which I will treasure as long as I live.

Dear Philip:

For my part, I consider it great honor that I was privileged to induct you into the Boy Scouts of America, and I must say that I found you a regular fellow, too. Stay that way and nothing will go to your head.

Sincerely,

Dwight D. Eisenhower ■

DAVID F. THORNTON
❧❧
Columbia University graduate / 1950

WHY I LIKE IKE

I graduated from Columbia in 1950, on a very hot day. My father and mother were seated in the rear of the audience of some 20,000 people out on Columbia's South Field. They had traveled all the way from Virginia to see me graduate, and now they were faced with the prospect of returning to the hotel without even meeting me after the ceremony. I was just one of many graduates, and the mass of humanity was too much to fight on such a sultry June afternoon.

When the academic procession had returned to Butler Library, father and mother started pushing through the crowd toward the nearest exit. Father was particularly gloomy – it had all seemed too cold and impersonal. He is accustomed to those wonderful small college affairs where everyone knows everyone else.

As they walked around the corner of the library, they came upon a crowd of people at one of the doors. Suddenly, Columbia's President Eisenhower appeared, cap and gown in hand, on his way back to his residence. Everybody smiled and the cameras started clicking.

"Go on over and say something to him," my mother

urged. She was well aware of father's unhappiness that afternoon. On the spur of the moment, father did what no one else – except mother – had thought to do. He walked over to Eisenhower, held out his hand, and said, "I certainly enjoyed your speech today, sir. You know, my son received his degree here today."

The famous infectious grin appeared on Ike's face, and it was evident that he appreciated my father's greeting.

"Well, isn't that fine," he glowed, grabbing father's hand firmly and warmly. "I bet you're mighty proud of him . . ."

They chatted for a few moments, and then Ike left. That was all there was to it: a simple courtesy, courteously received. But it provided the miracle touch which turned the day into a glorious and long-remembered occasion. ■

At the 1950 graduation ceremonies, Columbia
President Eisenhower presented an honorary
degree to the first Prime Minister of Pakistan,
Liaqat Ali Khan. In December 1959, Eisenhower
became the first U.S. President to visit that nation.

PHILIP YOUNG
❧❧

Dean, Columbia University Business School / 1950

WHY I LIKE IKE

Not many Americans know that Dwight D. Eisenhower, as president. of Columbia, conceived and established the first American Assembly, at Harriman, New York.

The aim of the Assembly is to throw impartial light on the major problems which confront America, so that our citizens can take effective steps toward solving the problems that hurt and trouble us most.

The idea had its roots in the World War II experiences of General Eisenhower. He was disturbed by the implications of the frequently repeated questions from soldiers: "What are we fighting for?" "Why am I overseas?" "Why does America care what a foreign dictator does?" Somewhere there seemed to be a failure in providing our people a clear understanding of the free way of life, its privileges as well as its duties.

I once asked General Eisenhower if he could tell me how the idea first occurred to him. He explained that on the numerous occasions when he spoke to the troops about why they were fighting, he tried to find a simple way to get the story across. Finally he found it.

He would pick out a specific individual in the group

and ask: "What are you going to do when you go home?"

In each case the reply was straightforward and definite: "I'm going to buy a filling station," or "I'm going to college," or "I'm going to build a new barn . . ."

"There is your answer," General Eisenhower would tell the troops. "In what other country of the world can you decide for yourself exactly what you want to do, with reasonable assurance of doing it? That's what you're fighting for."

In the American Assembly, where various groups come together for conferences, General Eisenhower may be leading us to an equally direct answer to the most profound and complex problems of our day. ■

Columbia University Arden House, site of the American Assembly.

In 1950, Eisenhower moved beyond the "100 acre" wheat farm in Kansas and bought a 189-acre cattle farm near Gettysburg, Pennsylvania. During his Presidency, he used the farm as a weekend retreat and a place to entertain visiting dignitaries. It became his full-time home in 1961.

The "residence" at the Gettysburg farm.

December, 1950: Eisenhower took a leave of absence from Columbia to become the first commander of SHAPE (Supreme Headquarters Allied Powers Europe), the first headquarters of the North Atlantic Treaty Organization (NATO).

During the next two years, his name was widely floated as a Republican presidential candidate.

LEONARD V. FINDER
✎✎

Publisher, Manchester (New Hampshire)
Union Leader / 1950

WHY I LIKE IKE

Shortly before General Eisenhower left to assume his duties as Commander-in-Chief of the NATO forces, I had occasion to visit him at his offices at Columbia University. During the course of our conversation, I inquired whether he had seen a nationally syndicated public opinion poll which, the night before, had announced its latest findings regarding presidential possibilities.

I told how the figures had shown that he led the entire field by a wide margin and that he had about as large a percentage as the next two runners-up combined. What was equally significant, I added, was that the results obviously swept across party lines as was shown by some of the other questions. Serious faced, General Eisenhower asked me solemnly, "Did the papers really say that?"

"Yes, they showed that you are the most popular man for the Presidency despite your unwillingness to become a candidate.

A sudden boyish grin flashed out as he exclaimed with irrepressible humor, "By golly, they sure are going to give me heck for this the next time they catch me in Washington."

When General Eisenhower was my guest in Manchester, New Hampshire, for the opening of our Community Forum, his visit began with a motorcade procession through part of the city. The approach to the City Hall, where he was to be given the key to the city, was jammed by thousands of persons. At last the cars could go no farther. People surrounded us so that driving became impossible.

As we sat there momentarily, General Eisenhower glanced about him. His eyes met those of a twelve-year-old boy, standing next to the car, eating popcorn. It seemed as though a message passed between two kindred spirits, for without a word, the boy held out his hand with the bag of popcorn, and the General gravely helped himself. As he ascended the speakers stand, he was still nonchalantly munching away.

The formalities over, he returned to the car. Just as a path was cleared so that we could move forward, the youngster silently thrust forward his hand again. Ike expected to take another handful, but the boy deposited the entire bag within his grasp, The General stared after the boy with a look of amazement. He turned to me and asked nearly incredulously, "Did you see that? He gave me his *whole* bag." Several times during the evening he repeated to me, "Just think, that boy gave up his whole bag of popcorn."

His modesty was such that it startled him to discover that a young American boy should be willing to present him with a whole bag of popcorn. ■

MARY A. HIGGINS
❧❧

"Woman in the Air Force" (WAF) / 1951

WHY I LIKE IKE

I was one of the first ten WAFS assigned to the SHAPE headquarters near Versailles. If you think Americans like Eisenhower, you should hear what the Europeans think about him. Judging by the people I met, including my roommates, who were Dutch and French girls, I would say he is the most popular American in the world if not the most popular man.

Why? I think it's because he is a walking advertisement for the democracy he sells. For example, when the new headquarters was dedicated, in July, 1951, great men of the many nations attended the ceremony. Eisenhower not only thought to invite the humble French tenant farmer who had owned the property, but he actually addressed him and said something about hoping we do as well with the property as he did. You can imagine how the French liked that.

My duties at SHAPE never involved working directly for Ike, but I saw him from time to time as he passed in the corridors. I was deeply impressed by the warm and friendly quality of his nature.

I was walking in the corridors with a British corporal

once after a Christmas address by Ike to the enlisted personnel. Ike came by conducting an entourage of VIPs through headquarters. He was talking to them, yet automatically as he passed he glanced at us and greeted us.

The corporal swelled with pride.

"Blimey, " he said, "that Ike's a wonderful man. If there were only more like him in the world we wouldn't be in such a bloody mess."

To me this is his most important asset. Ike always has time for the little man . . . a unique faculty which makes him a great man. ■

Supreme Headquarters Allied Powers Europe (SHAPE), 1951

SHAPE commander Eisenhower signing autograph for a soldier.

Photo by Henry Toluzzi. Used with permission from Stars and Stripes.

© 1951, 2012 Stars and Stripes

CECIL CARNES
᪥᪥

Radio Journalist, "Journey for Peace" / 1951

WHY I LIKE IKE

In January, 1951, I went to Europe to broadcast the radio program, "Journey for Peace." I met Ike for the first time when he stepped off the boat at Cherbourg for his fact-finding trip, before returning permanently to assume command of SHAPE (Supreme Headquarters Allied Powers Europe). It was his first time on French soil since the war. The boat docked at 3 a.m., and the mayor of the town was there with a party to escort the General to a champagne breakfast. Although he was tired and surprised, Ike took it in his stride and was a delight to his hosts.

From that time on I interviewed him, with a mike in my hands, all over Europe, from the snow of Oslo to the sun of Lisbon. Always, though there were many distractions, hundreds of people claiming his attention. When I came home I remember regretting that I did not get to know him better and thinking to myself that I bet the General would never remember me from Adam.

I did not see him again until a press conference in the little theatre in Abilene. I was standing down front with my back to the door, making arrangements, when I felt someone clobbering me on the back, and a booming voice said: "Hello and good morning and how the heck are you, Cecil?"

"Hello, General," I said, in amazement, "I'm surprised that you remember me."

"How could I forget," he replied. "You stuck that mike in my face in 14 different countries." ∎

Even though public interest in an Eisenhower candidacy was growing, Ike remained the reluctant candidate . . . until two WWII aviators—a Navy patrol plane pilot and a Marine fighter pilot—decided to give him a big nudge.

The "Citizens for Eisenhower" Bandwagon carried Ike-branded barrage balloons, the helium to fill them, "Ike" costumes for local volunteers, and a Jeep to lead the parade. The troupe would roll into a town at which Ike (traveling on his campaign train) would be speaking the next day, and put on a show to let everyone know who was coming!

The Bandwagon covered thirty-six states and 35,000 miles.

STANLEY M. RUMBOUGH
✍✍

Co-Founder, "Citizens for Eisenhower" / 1951

WHY I LIKE IKE

When Charlie Willis and I organized "Citizens for Eisenhower" in the Spring of 1951, Eisenhower was not even a candidate. Why would we enter the fray? Frankly, we did not like the quality of the politicians running the country and we felt that a man of integrity, ability, and humility might well become President. We did not even know whether he was a Democrat or Republican and we didn't care. In fact, we had never met him but we did know that he was immensely popular and greatly admired.

To complain is one avenue—to act is another. We had experience in starting and running several businesses, so we applied our entrepreneurial skills to setting up the organization, creating a headquarters—with a staff that grew to some 700 volunteers—and contacting friends around the country to become state chairmen and organize Eisenhower clubs in their states. A bit of market research revealed that most voters were more interested in Eisenhower, the man, than in the political issues of the day and thus we created what I truly believe to have been the most effective campaign slogan ever, "I Like Ike."

Our purpose was to convince Eisenhower that he

was wanted, and if he chose to run he had a very good chance of becoming President. We arranged petition drives and rallies. On February 8, 1952, the public-relations genius Tex McCrary staged a three-hour rally at Madison Square Garden and depended on us to fill the hall. We thought this would be difficult; because of an early evening sporting event in the Garden, this rally couldn't even start until 10 pm. The seating capacity was, as I recall, 16,000. Ike was already so popular that 25,000 fans showed up. McCrary put together a movie of the event, a not-so-subtle pleading for Ike to enter the race, and had the aviatrix Jacqueline Cochran fly it over to Ike's headquarters near Paris. She reported back that after he had viewed the film, Ike was so moved that he was in tears.

A month later, Ike won the New Hampshire primary---his name had been entered without his permission by Massachusetts Senator Henry Cabot Lodge. Jr.—and within a few days he agreed to be a candidate, with Lodge as campaign manager. By this time, "Citizens for Eisenhower" had been organized in 42 states, with hundreds of clubs and millions of volunteers.

We had met our first objective, and shifted to

direct campaign support—pointing, at first, toward the July Republican National Convention. We added some heavy hitters to our executive roster: Sidney Weinberg, a Democrat, became treaurer, and Mary Pillsbury Lord, a Republican, became co-chair with Walter Williams (chairman of the Council on Economic Development); Jock Whitney came aboard as chairman of Fundraising and Oveta Culp Hobby headed "Democrats for Eisenhower."

One early lesson learned: not many people showed up for Ike's first on-the-road campaign speech. Therefore, Citizens for Eisenhower opened an "Eisenhower Bandwagon Division," equipped with a branded truck and attention-grabbing "Ike" barrage balloons to float over a parade or a rally. There were bevies of attractive young ladies dubbed the "Ike Girls." The strategy was basic: we would drive into a town where Ike was scheduled to give a speech and make sure everyone knew he was coming.

There was much work to be done . . . to get the nomination and win an election. To skip ahead: Our proudest moment was after the election when Ike called Charlie and me into his office at the Commodore Hotel and said, "You two guys are responsible for my being here. I want you to come with me to Washington." ■

Charles Willis became head of the White House Personnel Office, Stanley Rumbough became head of the Office of Executive Branch Liaison.

HENRY McCAFFERTY

❧❧

New York City Policeman / 1952

WHY I LIKE IKE

I am a policeman assigned to the beat which takes in General Eisenhower's house at 60 Morningside Drive. Since he came back from Europe his house is marked for "special attention," and I stand about 25 or 30 feet from the door.

I've never talked with him, but it has been interesting observing the people coming and going. For one thing, when anyone is leaving, whether they are important or not, I notice he always tries to escort them to the door. This not only shows courtesy on his part – but it also gives me a chance to see him.

During those days when the delegates to the up-coming Republican Convention were calling on him his door would open almost every hour on the hour and he would walk out, and the photographers would snap pictures. There was a lot of handshaking and political chatter, and I always got the feeling that Ike was selling himself without humbling himself. For example, one delegate was playing the part of Prima Donna, just aching to be coaxed and wheedled.

Ike smiled at him and said: "Let your conscience be

your guide."

Most of all, though, I like the way kids take to him. Kids are pretty sharp at spotting a right guy. All the kids in the neighborhood hang around his house and run up to him when he comes to the door. One cute little red headed boy came to me all excited and yelled, "Hey, he rubbed my head!"

And Ike does rub. When a kid comes over to him he doesn't politely pat them like he has to but is afraid they have germs. He takes hold and gives them an affectionate massage. One neighborhood mother brought her daughter to see him, and her picture was taken with him and appeared on the front page of a Sunday paper. Now the kid comes back every day.

I'm not concerned with politics, but I have the feeling about Eisenhower that he's a man I'd like to know, really to know as a man. ■

Ike addressing troopers of the 82nd Airborne, about to parachute into France on D-Day, June 6, 1944.

CLARENCE ADAMY
❧❧

AMVETS National Service Director / 1952

WHY I LIKE IKE

Generals are schooled for war, and one often feels they may be insincere when they speak of peace. But I was there one day when General Eisenhower revealed the depth of his sincerity.

I handled arrangements for General Eisenhower's participation in the 82nd Airborne Division Convention in Chicago, just before the nominating convention.

On Saturday, the convention had a memorial luncheon to honor all members of the 82nd Division killed in action. At the table with him as his particular escort was the only living Medal of Honor holder of the 82nd Division, Leonard Funk, a former sergeant.

The Chaplain opened the memorial service in the darkened and hushed hall with a candle-light service. He gave a 20-minute eulogy about those who had so nobly served their country. Then a member of each unit stepped forward and, while the drums rolled in the background, read off the name of each man killed in action in his unit--a total of 498 men for the entire Division, including the recently added names of those in Korean units.

After the service the president of the 82nd Association introduced Leonard Funk. Len's speech was a brilliant expression of faith in the general. He told how on June 6, 1944, Eisenhower had a decision to make. A swamp just behind Omaha Beach had to be neutralized before the oncoming armies of men could land on the beaches, otherwise the whole invasion might fail. The general had no other choice but to drop the 82nd behind the lines. It was a terrible decision for a man to make. Ike not only made it, but had the courage to come personally to face the men he was sending to almost certain death.

Then Len introduced General Eisenhower.

He rose, and saluted the man in civilian clothes beside him, the Medal of Honor holder, Leonard Funk. Then he turned to face his audience.

Many of us may have forgotten some of what he said that day, but none of us will ever forget what he did that day. As he stood to speak, tears rolled freely and unashamed down General Eisenhower's cheeks. ∎

In the run-up to the July, 1952 Republican National Convention, a great number of delegates had been pledged to Ohio Senator Robert A. Taft. By the time Ike became an official candidate, Taft seemed to have a lock on the nomination. However, the enthusiasm of the amateur "Citizens for Eisenhower"—matched with the parliamentary skills of a group of professional Republicans who did not support Taft but favored Eisenhower and were led by Senator Henry Cabot Lodge, Jr.—won the day. Eisenhower was selected on the first ballot.

His Democrat opponent in the general election: Illinois Governor Adlai E. Stevenson. The race was on.

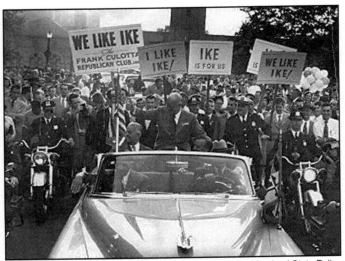

Credit: Maryland State Police

SHERMAN ADAMS
❧❧

Governor of New Hampshire / 1952

WHY I LIKE IKE

Right after the conventions, I spent three weeks living and working with General Eisenhower, preparing for the campaign. All of us worked extremely hard, but Ike set the pace.

Once he had three 16-hour working days in a row. At the end of the third afternoon he was about to leave and snatch a few minutes of much needed rest. On the way to his hotel room, a woman accompanied by three children put out her hand to greet him.

"I'm Mrs. So and So from Abilene," she said.

Ike immediately rose to the occasion, asked about her children, about other people in Abilene, listened intently to her answers, then asked more questions. His rest period was dented, but he had made a Kansas neighbor feel wonderful. Those of us who had been with him knew how badly he needed those few minutes.

On another occasion he actually got his rest, but at the same time gave me a chance to glimpse another facet of his amazing character.

After a particularly grueling session, Ike, his friend Aksel Nielsen of Denver, and I went fishing. It was great relaxation, but not a good fishing day for the General. Aksel Nielsen, on the other hand, had made a good catch.

"What's the secret, Aksel," Ike asked, "how come you're so far, ahead?"

"Well, Ike," Aksel answered, "you just fish in one pool. You have to get around. These trout are all up and down the stream."

Ike replied thoughtfully.

"You know, Aksel, that's the trouble with me in lots of things. I get to fishing in one pool and I have to try all the tricks of the trade, different ideas, new twists, as well as different pools. If I go away from there without a catch, and without trying everything, my conscience won't let me rest." ■

Governor Adams served as White House chief of staff, 1953-1958.

126

On November 4, 1952, Dwight D. "Ike" Eisenhower was elected 34th President of the United States. Ike came through with 442 electoral votes to Governor Stevenson's 89. He was the first Republican elected president since 1928, and he would serve two terms.

⤜⤛

The Presidential Inauguration, January 20, 1953, was preceded by a prayer service at Eisenhower's church, National Presbyterian. The pastor, Rev. Dr. Edward L. R. Elson, had been a colonel in the Army chaplain corps during the war, where he and Ike became friends. Dr. Elson offered a prayer:

"Grant unto Thy servant, Dwight David Eisenhower, now and henceforth, health of body, serenity of soul, clarity of insight, soundness of judgment, a lofty moral courage, a sanctified stewardship of office, and a constant and confident faith in Thee."

Inspired, Ike went back to his room in the Presidential Suite of the Statler Hotel and wrote out a prayer of his own, with which he began his inaugural address a short time later:

"My friends, before I begin the expression of those thoughts that I deem appropriate to this moment, would you permit me the privilege of uttering a little private prayer of my own. And I ask that you bow

Eisenhower inauguration, January 20, 1953.

your heads. Almighty God, as we stand here at this moment my future associates in the Executive branch of Government join me in beseeching that Thou will make full and complete our dedication to the service of the people in this throng, and their fellow citizens everywhere.

"Give us, we pray, the power to discern clearly right from wrong, and allow all our words and actions to be governed thereby, and by the laws of this land. Especially we pray that our concern shall be for all the people regardless of station, race or calling. May cooperation be permitted and be the mutual aim of those who, under the concepts of our Constitution, hold to differing political faiths; so that all may work for the good of our beloved country and Thy glory. Amen."

From left: Mamie Eisenhower, the President, the Reverend Billy
Graham, and Ike's pastor, the Reverend Dr. Edward Elson

ELEANOR ELSON HEGINBOTHAM

∾∾

Ike's pastor's daughter / 1953

WHY I LIKE IKE

I was in the awkward throes of junior high when Eisenhower was inaugurated. My father, the Rev. Dr. Edward L.R. Elson, had first come to know Eisenhower during his five years as an Army Chaplain in the European theater of the war. Eisenhower had decided to join National Presbyterian (formerly Covenant-First), the Washington DC church at which my father was pastor.

The friendship between my dad and his most famous parishioner opened my life, too, to frequent opportunities to see and chat with the Eisenhowers from the time of the inauguration until just after college, when my young groom and I left for a series of Foreign Service posts. During those years many world and church leaders came to our church and sat at our dinner table, among them a very young Billy Graham, who would work with my dad and others in such projects as congressional prayer breakfasts and who would be one of those recommending that Eisenhower join National Presbyterian.

A historic event occurred before the president could become a member of our church: he had to be baptized. As my dad told me, Eisenhower did not suddenly discover "faith." He was "steeped in biblical tradition and was brought up with daily Bible reading" and church attendance. However, the tradition of his devout River Brethren mother did not involve infant baptism. Throughout his Army career Ike attended services in non-denominational chapels. Ours was the first church he formally joined. Presbyterian membership assumes a re-affirmation of baptismal vows. Thus, ten days after his inauguration Eisenhower became the only president to be baptized while in office (by my father in a private, not public, service). In fact, a Catholic historian told my father that Eisenhower may have been the first head of state of any nation to be baptized since Clovis I, King of the Franks, in 496.

Later that day the new president stood up with other new members to become a member of National Presbyterian Church. From then on Mamie and Ike (my dad would never have called them that, respectful as he was), regularly attended services at National Presbyterian.

As a security measure and at the request of the Secret Service, the pastor's wife and four children filled out the pew. On most Saturday mornings the chief of Secret Service in the White House called my dad to advise how large the president's party would be on Sunday and therefore how many "pew fillers" might be in order. The Eisenhowers were escorted in by the head usher and escorted out by my dad during the last hymn.

Usually, only Mamie and Ike attended, but sometimes they brought grandchildren or friends; on one bright autumn day they brought the new Queen of England, an absolutely beautiful Elizabeth with her consort Prince Philip. On that occasion we sat right behind them.

On some of those Sundays when we shared a pew, this curious teen-ager (who perhaps was not fully involved in her father's prayer) could clearly observe the clasped hands of a president who obviously *was* deeply involved.

One Sunday in January, 1954, the president was so taken by the sermon that he asked for fifty copies to mail out to friends and colleagues. "The Mastery of Moods" dealt with the twin evils of an uncontrolled temper and a tendency to criticize rather than compliment, and how the love of God can be an antidote, a healer. Eisenhower sent the sermon, presumably a relevant one, to cabinet members, selected members of Congress, and some military leaders.

As the years progressed, the president's pastor, who also served as Chaplain of the U. S. Senate for a dozen years, visited Ike in the hospital, and took part in the president's funeral. Before that final event, however, on October 14, 1967---his 77th birthday---Eisenhower laid the cornerstone of a new home for National Presbyterian at Nebraska and Van Ness Streets.

In the windows of the Presidents' Chapel of that edifice, Eisenhower is one of six presidents depicted as exemplars of faith at work. That window shows another historic event: President Eisenhower signing the bill on June 14, 1954, inserting "under God" into the Pledge of Allegiance. Obviously my father believed that the president indeed lived *his* life "under God." ∎

Eleanor Elson Heginbotham, Ph.D and her (now-retired) Foreign Service Officer husband served in Liberia, Vietnam, and Indonesia. She has recently retired from her own career of teaching, most recently as Professor of English at Concordia University Saint Paul. She continues to write scholarly articles on American writers, especially Emily Dickinson.

Readers might be interested in the wider narrative presented in Dr. Elson's autobiography, Wide Was His Parish, *published in 1986.*

134

1962: Eisenhower encourages Gil Robinson on his run for
Congress, to represent a district in New York City.

GILBERT ROBINSON
❧❧

Youngest Member of the Administration / 1955

WHY I LIKE IKE

After one year of college I joined the Army, and, in 1947, was sent to Adak in the Aleutian Islands as a private. As noted earlier in this collection (page 52), Adak was an island with 5,000 soldiers and no women, trees or grass. It was not a place with any excitement. Therefore, when the Chief of Staff of the U. S. Army, the famous war hero General Eisenhower, came for a visit, it was a big thing—the man in charge of the Army reaching out to show his appreciation for the most isolated group of soldiers in the world.

One of my buddies was picked to be his driver. At one point, I took a jeep and went looking for where the General and his entourage might be. I kept my distance but when I saw the General's car parked outside the huge Quonset hut that was the mess hall I figured—since it was mid-morning—the General had stopped for some coffee.

I parked nearby and made my way to the General's car. My buddy and I had been chatting for a few minutes when someone shouted "Atten-hut!" and everyone popped to attention as General Eisenhower approached his car. I had brought my small Brownie camera with me. As Eisenhower passed right in front of me and bent to get into his car . . . I thought to myself . . . now or never

. . . and as I raised my camera I shouted."GENERAL!"
Eisenhower's host, the General in charge of the
Aleutians, was glaring at me as if he wanted to kill me.
General Eisenhower—wearing his famous Ike Jacket—
straightened up, and, seeing a young GI in working fatigues,
smiled that famous smile. (And, to his credit, when the
Commanding General of the Aleutians saw the camera,
he smiled also . . . whether reflex or good sense, I have no
idea.)

I had time only to snap one picture before he got in
the car. Then as the car sped off, I was chagrined to realize
that in the excitement of the moment I had forgotten to
salute. But that picture turned out to be one of the best I
have ever seen of Eisenhower.

Eight years later, I became the youngest appointee of
President Eisenhower's administration, as the Special
Assistant to Secretary of Commerce Sinclair Weeks.

Every month, the special assistants would have
dinner at the White House Mess with one of the Cabinet
officers. President Eisenhower would usually come out
for 15 minutes or so and mingle with the group. One
time, I engaged him in conversation and told him about
the picture I had taken of him on Adak. He said he

Photograph by Pvt. Gilbert A. Robinson, U. S. Army

remembered the trip. Then he said to me, "Why don't you send the picture over so I can sign it?" The photo now hangs in a place of honor in my home.

In 1962, I decided to make a run as a candidate for Congress from the west side of Manhattan. President Eisenhower took a special interest in my campaign, in part because the district included Columbia University and in part because of my work in his Administration; there were several thousand appointees working for the President, but, I believe, my role had been fixed in his mind because of that photograph.

I lost the election, but in the process earned an invitation to visit him at his farm in Gettysburg. As he had shown with his visit to the troops on far-away and out-of-the-way Adak, he was the most thoughtful and caring leader I have ever known. ■

140

Eisenhower portrait by J. Anthony Wills, courtesy of the
Eisenhower Memorial Commission

CARL W. REDDEL
᭜᭜

Brigadier General, USAF (Ret) and Executive Director,
Eisenhower Memorial Commission / 2012

WHY I LIKE IKE

What a privilege to reflect on these stories of Americans who knew and served General Eisenhower in different walks of life. Surprising to me was my personal response to the question posed to them by "Why I Like Ike."

Although I did not have the personal relationship with Ike that was the basis of their experiences, I found that I wanted to explain—to tell why I like Ike, just as these people did in their stories. Maybe this emotional impulse was one of the reasons Senator Ted Stevens said in 1999, upon receiving the Eisenhower Leadership Prize, "Where do I enlist?" He was speaking about the meaning of Eisenhower's impact and legacy for him as a combat veteran of World War II.

It's a strange feeling to take off a military uniform after 36-plus years of continuing service, which I did in 1999. Imagine what it was for Ike to do so in 1948, after 37 years of wearing the uniform and after having served as Supreme Commander of the Allied Forces in Europe in World War II and as Chief of Staff of the U. S. Army after the war. Not to mention his service as the first NATO commander.

Old enough to be both in high school and college

when Ike was president, I did not know that I would have the privilege of serving him in his memorialization, as the Executive Director of the Eisenhower Memorial Commission. I envy the personal pride of Kansans who celebrate their home-state hero, who in turn represented all of us so well. But why was his role in his own time, and now his legacy, so remarkable?

In explaining this, Gil Robinson has served all of us, as fellow-citizens, so well. He has given us an unusual chance to relate to a great American in purely human terms---not complex military, political or economic terms---but simply as one man or woman to another. It's not often you can touch a great American directly, or other great people in history, as another human being. Do we have similar stories to share about Churchill, De Gaulle, Montgomery, or Patton—as human beings?

I suggest that no leader in American history so completely embodied the American Dream, as Ike did. His special devotion to the dignity of the individual citizen of the United States transcended his own country. And he became the winning image of America to the world, gaining the respect, and even the affection, of people in every country he touched.

When President Eisenhower left Washington in 1959 to visit eleven countries in nineteen days, he exemplified and epitomized America for the whole world. People greeted him not only in the hundreds of thousands but also in the millions. As a result, *Time* magazine once again made him "Man of the Year" for 1960, having already done so in 1945. (His image was on the cover of *Time* eighteen times, sixteen times as the primary image.)

Ike's transcending humanity was evident throughout his presidency in both this country and abroad. He was indeed the most international of American presidents, the first to initiate the personal global diplomacy with which we have become so familiar in subsequent presidents.

Eisenhower was also the last president to pursue both freedom and security simultaneously, persistently, and pragmatically at the highest level for all Americans. He was passionate, until he drew his final breath as our last citizen-soldier president, about not wanting to sacrifice individual freedom for national security. Amazingly, he improved both freedom and national security by doing more for education, basic scientific research, and the transportation infrastructure (land, sea, air and space) of the United States than any other American leader, before or since, leading to peace and prosperity as the hallmarks of his presidency for eight years.

During those eight years, the style of his leadership

was marked by exceptional consensus and civility. He worked effectively with leaders of completely different political persuasion and public personality, such as the Majority Leader of the Senate, Senator Lyndon Johnson. The appeal of this style may have been one of the reasons for the formation across party lines of Citizens for Eisenhower, America's single most successful independent political movement in U.S. history, which led to Ike's election as president.

So, if Gil and those others who have provided the anecdotes in this book are right, and I believe they are, Ike is the most luminary embodiment we have of the success of what our founding fathers set about to achieve. We are a country in which a common man from ordinary circumstances could realize a remarkable personal destiny, because he received a sound basic public education and was imbued by his family and community with the burning desire to better himself. Is there a single better lesson for all of us today?

This is IKE. This is America's story.

Made in the USA
Charleston, SC
13 July 2012